Hap♡ W9-BNP-427

... Wait til we tell
Pete what you did
this weekend ...

Love Ben & Jess
xx

Irish Shades Of Grey

Irish Shades of Grey

The 500 BEST Tweets from the

#IrishShadesOfGrey Twitter Phenomenon

Edited by Paul Duggan

NEW ISLAND

IRISH SHADES OF GREY
First published 2012
by New Island
2 Brookside
Dundrum Road
Dublin 14
www.newisland.ie

PRINT ISBN: 978-1-84840-210-2

British Library Cataloguing Data. A CIP catalogue record
for this book is available from the British Library

Typeset by New Island Books
Cover design by Martin Gleeson.
Printed by ScandBook AB

New Island received financial assistance
fromThe Arts Council (An Comhairle
Ealaíon), Dublin, Ireland

10 9 8 7 6 5 4 3 2 1

To Isobel Charlotte, for when you are older. You may outgrow my lap but never my heart.

Introduction

The Irish suffer from a striking inability to talk frankly about sex, whether on television, in literature or just amongst ourselves. When it comes to discussing sex and sexuality, everything is a wink and a nudge or a double entendre, undoubtedly a legacy of our Catholic heritage. We were taught when growing up that sex was an abomination; a dirty act and a mortal sin that will damn us all to hell. An act so terrible that you should only do it with your husband or wife, preferably with the lights turned off and a hole cut in the sheets. What we are much more comfortable doing instead, though, is laughing and joking about sex.

There was a time in Ireland when we were much more likely to ban raunchy books than to read them. It is all the more remarkable, then, that the global phenomenon that was E.L. James' *Fifty Shades of Grey* was as successful as it was here in Ireland. For weeks, the airwaves were awash with tales of Irish mammies, whose insatiable appetite for the trilogy became hotter than the immersion left on all night, much to the bemusement and sometimes horror of Irish men, who, while wailing and gnashing their teeth about the quality of the literature, were afraid deep down of being replaced by a book.

Take one bored Cork man, one Monaghan man bemoaning the standard of erotic literature and one slow news day, add a dash of social media, and you have quite the deadly combination. The ensuing conversation created the twitter hashtag #IrishShadesOfGrey, to which I tweeted the following narrative:

'I'd like to lob the gob,' he whispers darkly.

She thinks to herself, I'm shaking in me boots and he hasn't he even touched me.

His lips part, ready, he's coiled to strike, my insides churn like I've just drank sour milk.

She can smell his breath on her, he smells like an ashtray and 20 pints of Bulmers.

The Irish catholic guilt thing sweeps over her. He gazes upon her like a Big Mac about to be devoured.

'I normally don't do this on the first night,' she whispers. He wonders where he has heard that before.

She gasps as his lips meet hers. She feels all moist and gooey inside, like a Cadbury's Creme Egg....

She grasps his throbbing hurley.

He prepares to storm the gates of her love fort with his battering ram....

'Do you have protection?' she whispers. 'I've a baseball bat in the back, but those lads haven't been round here in a while.'

'No, I mean for yer willy! The chemist goes to the Legion of Mary with me Da, so I'm not on anything....'

'Feck,' he seethes. 'The rhythm method was proven by the TV show myth-busters...' he claims.

She fights back a wave of catholic guilt. 'You can have a bit of a feel,' she whispers....

He's aching all over, but it could be from the wild beating he took from the bouncers earlier.

He wants her ... He lobs the gob, again she writhes beneath his slobbery kiss like she's being mauled by an Irish wolfhound.

They break the passionate, spaghetti-like embrace ... 'I have something to tell you,' he moans. She looks on nervously.

'I'm a member of Fianna Fáil,' he wails ... She recoils in horror ... But she remembers what her friend had told her about him ... She is reminded of her friend's tale of his prowess ... 'Sure he's hung like a horse and goes like a sewing machine … He's not a Singer though....'

She doesn't care about his Fianna Fáil past, she wants him. She hasn't felt this way since the under-16s got to the county final.

'Make love to me,' she whispers. 'I don't make love, I will ride ya like you're stolen,' he grunts.

She knew his pedigree. He was from the kinda place where the men were men and the sheep were nervous....

He lobs the gob. He drops the hand. 'What is that?' he roars. 'Tis a chastity belt....' 'Hang on, I've an angle-grinder.'

He was grunting now. Sparks flew, and it got warmer as he cut away at the chastity belt with his angle-grinder.

Irish Shades of Grey

Are you kinky?' he asks. 'What do you want me to do?' she says. 'Put an orange in your mouth & a bag on yer head.'

'You love me,' she whispers. His eyes widen, his mouth opens, like he's been hit with a hurley by Henry Shefflin. 'Ehhh, of course I do.' *awkward silence*

Both naked now, taking comfort in the fact that not even the Hubble telescope could penetrate the darkness.

He groans, grunts and sweats like a gravedigger. She yells, screams and moans like she means it.

'How was it for you?' he asks.

'Best 3 minutes of my life,' she whispers demurely

Twitter, being the medium of instant news, took over, and people all over Ireland and the world tweeted their own versions of #IrishShadesOfGrey. Irish household names such as *The Late Late Show*'s musical director Jim Sheridan, broadcasters Hector Ó hEochagáin and Will Leahy and 2FM's Ruth Scott all added their own versions. Over the following weeks, most national and international news outlets covered #IrishShadesOfGrey, and the internet sensation that followed.

This book would not have been possible without the help and advice of John McGuirk, AJ O'Flaherty and Anne-Marie O'Connor and the good folk at New Island Books, especially Eoin Purcell.

Royalties from the sale of Irish Shades Of Grey will be donated to a charity chosen by the readers. Visit www.newislandnews.com/royaltydecision to cast your vote!

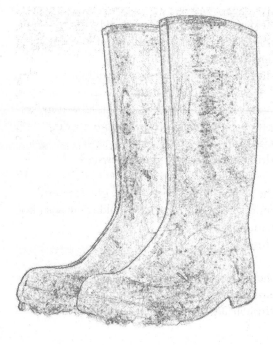

Irish Shades of Grey

As they had hot, intense, orgasmic sex, Mick
cried 'Moan, baby, Moan!' 'OK,' said Mary,
'That kitchen needs painting!!'
#IrishShadesOfGrey | joeman42

He slipped his hand under the red silk. 'You're so
beautiful in that dress.' 'Feck off, it was only a
euro in Penneys!'
#IrishShadesOfGrey | LeanneWoodfull

I drank in the tightness of its skin. How firm, yet
soft, it was. He breathed, wild, into my ear.
'Can't bate new schpuds.'
#IrishShadesOfGrey | PaudieNewstalk

She pouted and begged, 'Please, give it to me,'
but the teller at Ulster Bank couldn't say what her
account balance was.
#IrishsShadesOfGrey | phoebz4

She woke up to the smell of the underwear of 10
boys. Being a *Bean an Tí* was tough work now!
#IrishShadesOfGrey | seanboneill

'Spit on me, Dickie!' she roared. Mr Rock duly
obliged. Sweet Jesus, it felt good.
#IrishShadesOfGrey | NightLord2009

'UlsterBank! UlsterBank!' she screamed, but he continued to screw her. Mary and Tom's safety word had failed catastrophically….
#IrishShadesOfGrey | SheenaMadden

'You're the dirtiest bitch I've ever met in my entire life,' he told Bubu, after catching the dog trying to fuck the cat.
#IrishShadesOfGrey | iGarageIreland

The crack of the whip made her quiver with excitement. The thoughts of all those men looking at her … one furlong to go!
#IrishShadesOfGrey | daithi_g

As she ran her hands thru the rich mane of his hair, Alice asked herself what she was doing in the lions' enclosure at the zoo
#IrishShadesOfGrey | Derekfallon

Gently, he caressed her plump tits. Then, in silence, he opened the aviary door and replaced them.
#IrishShadesOfGrey | pjmccluskey

He entwined his fingers in her long, soft hair and grew excited. 'I'll give yi a tonne for this pie ball mr'
#IrishShadesOfGrey | Make_UpMistress

Her bed was warm and inviting, but he could take no more hard rubbing, so he headed out the cat flap instead.
#IrishShadesOfGrey | piperpaw

His enormous cock pulsated wildly in her hand. 'Jesus,' said she, 'the hens won't know what hit them.'
#IrishShadesOfGrey | Mal1905

'I'm caked in manure!' Seanie said. Bridie felt a tingle inside. She loved it when he talked dirty.
#IrishShadesOfGrey | oconnellbrian

It lay cold, limp and grey in his hand. He was embarrassed. 'Jays,' Eleanor gasped, 'Where did that mackerel come from?'
#IrishShadesOfGrey | AnFearRuaGAA

'Just go for it, pin her against the wall and stick it in.' Tom appreciated the advice, he had never dosed a calf before.
#IrishShadesOfGrey | lauraaaah

My body was explored then it was licked, sucked and bitten. Moments later I was sore and itchy all over. FECKIN MIDGET BITES
#IrishShadesOfGgrey | janeen_short

'Oh Paddy, that cock is grand!' said Aine, who was after a rooster to treat her few hens.
#IrishShadesOfGrey | kevism

Pat stroked the sweat from her heaving sides, loosening the sticky leather strap. This filly wants it firmer, he thought
#IrishShadesOfGrey | Damsonz

'Red room of pain? Come here to me, you pup,' I said, 'and I'll show you a red room of pain!' The nerve of him!
#IrishShadesOfGrey | CelineKiernan1

The Postman's breath shortened when he saw Mrs Whelan's wet pussy ... 'Fucken cat's out in the rain again,' said he.
#IrishShadesOfGrey | laineyhughes

His fingers delicately caressed the body he knew he'd soon get to ravage. It was time to dismantle that e-voting machine.
#IrishShadesOfGrey | mynameisMrSnrub

'Give it to me, give it to me!' he roared aggressively. Some days Mary hated working at Ulster Bank.
#IrishShadesOfGrey | Kitsgirl1

Ann was frustrated it was in and out, and in again, and nothing. ATM was out of order again
#IrishShadesOfGrey | ShaneFitz1991

Finally here, she received it excitedly; handling it in a firm grip, cultivated by years of experience with dole cheques
#IrishShadesOfGrey | PhilipSpain

'Harder, Harder!' she roared as she anticipated climax. Larry Gogan searched for difficult qs b4 the 60 secs were up
#IrishShadesOfGrey | finianmoran

'I can't help it, it's shrinking,' Sean cried into his pillow. Brid realized she should never ask an economist about GDP
#IrishShadesOfGrey | KevinDenny

I feel bad sometimes, but she's so easy tis hard to say no. Best thing is I do none of the work. Tis grand on the dole
#IrishShadesOfGrey | iPeadar

'Let me see what's inside your love box,' he asked. Quietly, Mary cursed herself for ringing Psychic Wayne again.
#IrishShadesOfGrey | philipnolan1

Pat couldn't take his eyes off those tits, he spent
hours watching them, he truly was addicted to
the *Mooney Show* webcam
#IrishShadesOfGrey | kencurtin

She bit her lip when he revealed his Hadron
Collider & climaxed when he released sub-
atomic particles over her Higgs Bosom
#IrishShadesOfGrey | PaddyofNazareth

She lay down, he softly whispered that this would
be the longest, hardest & deepest experience of
her life. Damn Recession
#IrishShadesOfGrey | kbkevinbyrne

She was red in the face, panting and moaning.
She groaned, 'Me feckin wages still aren't in
Ulster Bank!'
#IrishShadesOfGrey | niamhhassell

The Minister's ejaculations became more forceful
with each repetition. God, how she loved
listening to *Oireachtas Report*
#IrishShadesOfGrey | kavatarz

The room smouldered with suppressed tension.
Joan flinched as Eamon growled 'You'll never get
my job' #laboursway
#IrishShadesOfGrey | PaddyJoeMcGilly

The thoughts of seeing some wood made her
heart race and perspiration broke out on her
upper lip, *Frontline* was on soon
#IrishShadesOfGrey | SuBuckley

We were from two different worlds. He liked
Dutch Gold, I liked Druids. But that night, we
made love through vodka.
#IrishShadesOfGrey | JamieCummins_

When he'd finished she smiled at him, a creamy
white line across her top lip. 'Your Irish Coffees
are the best, Finbar.'
#IrishShadesOfGrey | cecilbdeholy

… and she greedily swallowed his ginger nuts,
having dunked them in a cup of Barry's tae.
#IrishShadesOfGrey | colinodwyer

As she ran her tongue over the hard, moist head
she thought 'Didn't Fat Frogs used to be bigger?'
#IrishShadesOfGrey | justysir

Breathing softly, Mary eased her way down. She
was ready for pleasure. *Click*. The kettle was
now boiling.
#IrishShadesOfGrey | PaChalkWhite20

Bridie approached it, let her inhibitions go & let it spray all over her face. Ya couldnt bate a tin o'cola with a schtick
#IrishShadesOfGrey | shaneok87

He couldn't hold it in. He opened his mouth & let out a deep moan. Séamus had well & truly burnt his tongue on his tea.
#IrishShadesOfGrey | imsodoherty

He kissed her & lowered his hands down her curves. She was as moist as he imagined. He laid her on the table. His pint.
#IrishShadesOfGrey | JohnDeSolps

He pushed harder, squeezing deeper into the tight gap.... 'Can I have 2 Guinness and a Heineken?' he shouted at the barman
#IrishShadesOfGrey | mkellyirl

He shoved it down her throat, but she struggled and did her best to resist. She swallowed it but sure nobody likes Calpol.
#IrishShadesOfGrey | LyndaInNYC

He turns to look at her with his piercing eyes and then whispers heavily in her ear, 'Would ye ever make us a cup of tae?'
#IrishShadesOfGrey | Shinnybeans

Irish Shades of Grey

He was enthralled by the vision of beauty before him and knew that he couldn't resist. He loved Guinness that much
#IrishShadesOfGrey | Ladyfuckwit

Her fingers were gently circling the top when it suddenly erupted all over her. 'Who shook the f**king Fanta?'
#IrishShadesOfGrey | br1ank

His cream spurted on her face & hair. Sighing, she wondered if there was more to head than blowing on a pint of Guinness
#IrishShadesOfGrey | Greadyfarmer

'I'll never fit all that,' gasped Mary excitedly, 'it's too much!' 'Okay,' replied Sean, 'I'll put the Stella back'
#IrishShadesOfGrey | coriordan

'I'll take three more,' she said, with a dirty grin. She couldn't wait to get them in her mouth. Well, it was last orders….
#IrishShadesOfGrey | Taxiforwoody

'I'm sorry, I don't usually pay for this….' He was right. John always disappeared when it was his round.
#IrishShadesOfGrey | McCarthikus

It was the moment of truth: spit or swallow?? The creamy froth above her lip as she indulged in her first pint of Guinness
#IrishShadesOfGrey | AlanJDuncan

It was warm going down her throat & the horrible taste shocked her. Gráinne wouldn't be drinking Dutch Gold ever again.
#IrishShadesOfGrey | LyndaInNYC

Licked his lips softly, waitin for this for a long time, he closed his eyes as he got the 1st taste of his lovely Guinness
#IrishShadesOfGrey | onyerbike69

Majella licked her lips and took it all in her mouth. She loved a good bicky wit her tae.
#IrishShadesOfGrey | ShannonnClarkee

Mary loved a stiff one. The feel of it on her lips, that warm liquid sliding down her throat. 'Good whiskey,' she said.
#IrishShadesOfGrey | Grahamer14

Mary staggered into her room, trembling. She lay down and realised just how drunk she was after Siobhán's house party
#IrishShadesOfGrey | DRUMorDIE

Irish Shades of Grey

Mary was anxious, it was so long since her last
one. She swallowed hard and her face grimaced.
Tequila was a bad idea.
#IrishShadesOfGrey | ornatoolbox

'My god…' he said, 'you're… so … tight!' 'Feck,'
she thought. 'I really need to get my round in.'
#IrishShadesOfGrey | clicky_here

'Oh god, I needed that,' she said, after the first
drop hit the back of her throat. 'I've been
hanging for a cup of tea.'
#IrishShadesOfGrey | ocultado

Opening the zip, she reached in, feeling around
before her hands found a comforting hardness.
Crouching tiger hidden naggin
#IrishShadesOfGrey | stephenfinn3

'Put it in again, and again, and again,' she urged.
'Tae's no good if you can see the bottom of
the mug.'
#IrishShadesOfGrey | clogheentipp

Salty from being left dry so long, Mick's fingers
slipped and Brenda's rashers were left hanging
#IrishShadesOfGrey | fiddlyfecker

She can smell his breath on her, he smells like an
ashtray and 20 pints of bulmers....
#IrishShadesOfGrey | IsMiseAnCoinin_

She could feel it coming. She looked up, and steam was everywhere, then she heard that beautiful noise. The kettle was boiled
#IrishShadesOfGrey | againstthewall2

She had it gripped well before she twisted, flicked and used her teeth, before realising it wasn't a twisty cap Miller
#IrishShadesOfGrey | hpcreep

She kept pulling Patrick's handle and watching it pour froth. The last thing Mary wanted to do was change a barrel.
#IrishShadesOfGrey | mkejohn

She turned around, 'spoons?', pressed hard and then squeezed every last drop out of his Lyons tea bags
#IrishShadesOfGrey | kevindoyle78

She was happy to swallow, not spit it out. It tasted so nice and she sucked and wished for more. Yep, Nescafé mocho.
#IrishShadesOfGrey | 68Murfy

'Sorry, this doesn't usually happen,' John said, ashamed. But there was no excuse for not having a working kettle
#IrishShadesOfGrey | ShaneFitz1991

The golden droplets showered all over her … it was mighty craic shaking a can of Fanta before you opened it
#IrishShadesOfGrey | susankilkenny

The heat between them was intense as their insatiable desire culminated in a high-pitched screech: 'Kettle's boiled!'
#IrishShadesOfGrey | SeleneAlford

The white cream oozed out of the 6" vessel and trickled slowly over her fingers. Babs nearly dropped her pint of Guinness
#IrishShadesOfGrey | luvs2spooge84

White saltiness dribbled voluptuously down Bridget's chin. She gasped ecstatically. Nothing like buttermilk on a hot day.
#IrishShadesOfGrey | cmccrudden

Writhing with joy, she let the head pass between her lips. 'Sure and begorrah,' she cried, 'That's a feckin good Guinness!'
#IrishShadesOfGrey | onlyalexhayden

He loved her. No other man had ever touched her, but now he could only watch on while this guy vibrated her for the NCT
#IrishShadesOfGrey | kencurtin

She was sweating, in and out, in and out. He was turning red.… In and out again.… Finally, he said, 'I'll park it myself'
#IrishShadesOfGrey | Rustphil

After the steamy, wild romp, Mary asked Pat to turn off the light. Pat closed the car door.
#IrishShadesOfGrey | duckbox

Deirdre moaned, clutching the dashboard, as it got longer and longer. M50 tailbacks were a nightmare on a Friday.
#IrishShadesOfGrey | aimseroo

'Hands off!' he cried. 'It may be covered in cigarette burns and held together with rope, but that Ford Cortina is all mine'
#IrishShadesOfGrey | CelineKiernan1

He slowly eased into her space watching her expectation reach its climax. 'Now that's how you park a feckin car,' he said
#IrishShadesOfGrey | MarkSidmk

He squeezed in slowly, but it was so much tighter than he expected. Parking is always a disaster in Stephen's Green
#IrishShadesOfGrey | LyndaInNYC

He waited until she was almost there before
pulling out. He loved getting one over on the
parking inspector of a Monday
#IrishShadesOfGrey | Lorna_Sleek

Mary never had one quite like this. Big. Sturdy.
Powerful. The new Land Rover.
#IrishShadesOfGrey | IamBootsy

Paddy slipped it up her rear entrance quickly,
before she could moan … he knew she preferred
parking round the back
#IrishShadesOfGrey | Glamourpussmamo

Sean strained as he positioned his firm shaft into
place. Hooking up his caravan to his Land Rover
was tricky.
#IrishShadesOfGrey | GeordieWalrus

Sinead mounted it and she could feel it
throbbing, vibrating between her legs. You just
can't bate a Massey Ferguson!
#IrishShadesOfGrey | Juno_Macloon

SWEET MOTHER O JAYSUS YER RIGHT
UP ME ARSE – just another day on the M5.
#IrishShadesOfGrey | Shannon2Wel

Be jaysus 'tis a long one!' Mary exclaimed, as
Mickey showed her his freshly dug parsnip.
#IrishShadesOfGrey | JHutchieLaw

Theres no room, I'll need to push it back.' 'Ah I'm uncomfortable now,' said Biddy, as Ted adjusted the front seat of the car
#IrishShadesOfGrey | kbkevinbyrne

'You just have another inch to get in,' he assured her as she struggled. Maybe they needed a roof-rack for the surfboard.
#IrishShadesOfGrey | iGarageIreland

Hot & sweaty, as the juices flowed, salty yet sweet, no one but Mary could boil cabbage this good.
#IrishShadesOfGrey | joeman42

'For the love of god, why did Patrick always come so damn quickly?' thought Mary as she served leek & potato soup.
#IrishShadesOfGrey | Glamourpussmamo

He fondled the fruits. 'Dem's peaches, not Mickeys,' cried the Moore St. vendor, 'dey don't get bigger by feelin em.'
#IrishShadesOfGrey | clogheentipp

He fondled, prodded, pushed, parted, tried to insert, but he just couldn't get the fig into the fig roll.
#IrishShadesOfGrey | thomasjstamp

Irish Shades of Grey

He knew her weak spot, and he would make her beg for more. Rasher sandwiches always had that effect on her
#IrishShadesOfGrey | Ladyfuckwit

He ran his tongue around the chocolate rim. Oooh, the pleasure. #dunking
#IrishShadesOfGrey | MirthMaker1

He took one of her fingers and put it into his mouth and sucked slowly, then reached for another … LEAVE MY KITKAT ALONE!
#IrishShadesOfGrey | genieoregan

He watched the juices flow. The smell he craved all day. He licked his lips as Mary poured the gravy over his Sunday Roast.
#IrishShadesOfGrey | onyerbike69

'I'll never fit that in me gob!' she squealed, looking at it in his hand. 'Try,' he said, passing the giant Tolberone to her.
#IrishShadesOfGrey | front_whine

It's so big, she thought. How will I get it in my mouth? Then she realised she could cut the jumbo batter sausage.
#IrishShadesOfGrey | ashneary

May leaned her exhausted body against the bonnet and glanced at John. 'Get the fecking crunchies out of the feckin car'
#IrishShadesOfGrey | emma_janer

She gazed at him longingly, dreaming of a 69 … But her personal trainer said 'not a hope of Chinese take away.'
#IrishShadesOfGrey | LiamButler3

She slowly sucked the long length deep into her throat. She loves those pasta strings.
#IrishShadesOfGrey | coffpau

She squeezed the two hairy balls firmly, and the man grimaced. 'Those kiwis are ripe, Madam,' he said.
#IrishShadesOfGrey | luludog19

Surveying the tumescent bulb glistening in the light, a smile played on his lips. God he was proud of his prize onions.
#IrishShadesOfGrey | BufordTJ

The white liquid was all over her hands, and slowly trailed down her leg. 'Ya shouldn'a dropped the milk, Biddy. Bad luck.'
#IrishShadesOfGrey | ImogenGeek

'6 inches,' he said, smiling. It wasn't too big; it
was just right. She put on her gloves and
continued. Subway was his favourite
#IrishShadesOfGrey | kylem17

After steamy, passionate time together and he
took her for grub, he treated her to the Euro
saver menu in McDonald's
#IrishShadesOfGrey | FredSharkey

And she knew he was satisfied as she swallowed
his creamy mixture. John was really proud of his
mash spuds
#IrishShadesOfGrey | ShaneFitz1991

André slowly exposed the softness that lay
beneath the golden cover. Then, firmly, he put a
bit of butter on the spuds.
#IrishShadesOfGrey | IanFlavin

Ann-Marie swirled the balls around in her mouth
tenderly. 'You can't beat a bull's-eye,' she said.
#IrishShadesOfGrey | IpCollins

As he pushed into the soft centre with his finger
and the smooth liquid ran out, he knew he had
found the perfect fried egg
#IrishShadesOfGrey | lorraineritchie

Paul Duggan

As Mary wiped the white substance from her face, she turned to Tom & moaned, 'These mayonnaise sachets are a nightmare to open'
#IrishShadesOfGrey | howieyanow

Aunt Mary once told me about how they rolled together and formed something magical, getting the fig in the figroll
#IrishShadesOfGrey | ShaneFitz1991

Breda was surprised as the cream suddenly splattered her chest. Eating eclairs can be so messy.
#IrishShadesOfGrey | 86thLeinster

Bríd takes a deep breath and groans sensually. 'Aww, I love four fingers,' she whispers as she unwraps her KitKat
#IrishShadesOfGrey | horan_james

Bulbous, red, shiny & ripe. No matter what position she took, that stubborn radish just wouldn't budge from the soil
#IrishShadesOfGrey | cairotango

'Clonakilty sausages would be the death of her' I AM CRYING
#IrishShadesOfGrey | iamleigh_hi

Irish Shades of Grey

C'mere timme, would ya like a lick of my 99
like? #RebelShadesOfGrey
#IrishShadesOfGrey | TomMcCarthyCork

'Do you want 2 fingers or 3?' he whispered to her
… 'I want the whole KitKat ya greedy bastard!'
replied Maude.
#IrishShadesOfGrey | Lorna_Sleek

'Do you want a finger?' asked John. 'I'll just have
a bag of Taytos; I'm not in the mood for
chocolate,' replied Mary
#IrishShadesOfGrey | sherlockodile

Gazing at her bazookas, he wanted them, he
needed them. He could almost taste them. 'Buy
your own chewing gum,' she snarled.
#IrishShadesOfGrey | Derekfallon

Greedily, she closed her mouth around it. Some
white goo appeared at the edges of her mouth.
How she loved eclairs!
#IrishShadesOfGrey | mangofever

'Harder! Faster! Harder!' she moaned. That was
the last time she would get Anto to make the
mash for dinner....
#IrishShadesOfGrey | finchcaddy

Having watched the sheath pulled onto the shaft, and his meat filling it completely, Bridie bought a pound of sausages.
#IrishShadesOfGrey | Mal1905

He asked if she could handle more than one finger. She said she preferred HobNobs or a purple Schnack with the tea.
#IrishShadesOfGrey | Barsacq

He gazed hungrily at her firm breasts, contemplating the price. Nah, I'll get a cheaper chicken in Lidl.
#IrishShadesOfGrey | chris_mcginley1

He gently wrapped his lips around it. It was moist and warm. Possibly the best mince pie he'd ever had
#IrishShadesOfGrey | Andrew_Begley

He grasped the firm melons as she caressed the meatballs. Come to the English Market for good eating! #RebelShadesOfGrey
#IrishShadesOfGrey | TomMcCarthyCork

He gripped it firmly. She licked its full length, liking the feeling in her mouth. Sue loved a red devil icepop on a hot day
#IrishShadesOfGrey | feelingcrap

Irish Shades of Grey

He groaned with desire as she guided it longingly towards her mouth. Finally! This season's new potatoes were here!
#IrishShadesOfGrey | ColleenRossiter

He had the look of a savage in his eyes. She didn't know bacon & cabbage could do that to a man
#IrishShadesOfGrey | theskinnydoll

He looked at her satisfied face & said 'you were hungry for that.' She glanced at her empty plate, it was a nice lunch!
#IrishShadesOfGrey | MariaMcM1

He pushed his fingers through the opening, rubbing the inside slowly. The last Tayto crumbs were to be savoured
#IrishShadesOfGrey | quaidrayn

He ran his fingers deep into the sweet centre of the pink. Nothing would come between John and this Mikado
#IrishShadesOfGrey | CaptainSteveFTW

He slowly slid his middle finger up inside the soft, wet entrance. 'Yes, the chicken is now ready for the stuffing, mum!'
#IrishShadesOfGrey | JVistaTweets

He smiled at her. She hadn't seen one so big in years. They just couldn't get bags of Mega Meanies in Mullingar any more.
#IrishShadesOfGrey | Sean_is_Deadly

He stirred her, back and forth, round and round, his sausage began to rise … he knew then the coddle was ready
#IrishShadesOfGrey | Wilhelmsson79

He teased her with the huge vegetable … 'This big turnip looks like your head' he said.
#IrishShadesOfGrey | mickcreagh

He was torn between his love of Kimberley and her sister Mikado
#IrishShadesOfGrey | TheBrianDuggan

Her beefy loins were reaching boiling point, it was getting steamy. Theresa knew her stew was overcooked
#IrishShadesOfGrey | RianMac

Her eyes lit up as he pulled up outside Supermac's in his Opel Corsa with the full body kit. He knew how to spoil a girl
#IrishShadesOfGrey | Jewlieann

I'm going to beat you til you're broken,' he whispered … as he whisked the eggs with vigor
#IrishShadesOfGrey | 021sarahg

Irish Shades of Grey

Joan gasped as she held Mick's mouli, amazed by its power despite its size. 'My soup has never been so smooth!' she cried.
#IrishShadesOfGrey |Ionmhain

How was it for you?' Maura sighed. 'I've had better,' replied Jim. 'Don't buy their steak again, Superquinn's is nicer.'
#IrishShadesOfGrey | HearneAoife

Her face, contorted with pleasure, took the dark object from her mouth one last time. 'Can't bate a good Flake,' she said.
#IrishShadesOfGrey | Brynmorbeer

His pearly white goo trickled slowly down her chin. 'I shouldn't have shared me Creme Egg with me burd,' cursed Sean
#IrishShadesOfGrey | petesonearth

His tongue thrust deep into the tight, wet space … the last bit of chocolate in a Cornetto is always such a bitch to reach.
#IrishShadesOfGrey | abbygreen3

'How many fingers?' he whispered in her ear. 'FUCKIN FOUR!' she screamed. He unwrapped the KitKat & gave her the entire bar
#IrishShadesOfGrey | KarlsTRIPattoni

It had gotten from soft to hard in a matter of seconds. Mags found it tough work boiling eggs.
#IrishShadesOfGrey | luvs2spooge84

It was hard when he slid it carefully into the warm wetness, it was soft when he took it out … the biscuit in his tea
#IrishShadesOfGrey | cacytrayboo

It was pink … yielding … and he tasted that saltiness on the tip of his tongue. God, he loved her hang sangwidges
#IrishShadesOfGrey | DickCheeseman

It was so wet! Jim was surprised when it started to get limp. Mary told him not to leave his biscuit in his cuppa 2 long
#IrishShadesOfGrey | MaresD

'Just spread those legs and stuff it in … yeah, just do it now!' she exclaimed. And it was the best Christmas Turkey yet.
#IrishShadesOfGrey | kbkevinbyrne

'Lets shove something triangular into us,' said Jim. Mary thought 'I love a good Toblerone after his golf trips.'
#IrishShadesOfGrey | Kitsgirl1

Irish Shades of Grey

'Lob it in to me, boss!' roared Ted. Next time, thought Larry, just park closer to the feckin drive-thru window.
#IrishShadesOfGrey | FachtnaK

Maire gagged, opening her mouth as wide as it would allow, saltiness seeping in. She loved a bag of Meanies
#IrishShadesOfGrey | mizz_adventure

Majella licked her lips and took it all in her mouth. She loved a good biccie wit her tay.
#IrishShadesOfGrey | MrsYule

Mary felt him come up behind her. She squirmed with delight. The Whippy van was early tonight....
#IrishShadesOfGrey | Rayzore

Mary heard the familiar sound of a foil packet being torn open and she got excited … She always loved a bag of Tayto's
#IrishShadesOfGrey | MrLaurenceKirby

Mary screamed all over the house, 'Kevin…! Kevin…!!' Kevin moaned, 'I'm coming!!' His tea was on the table.
#IrishShadesOfGrey | RianMac

Mary swallowed eagerly as her mouth filled with creamy white goodness. She fecking loved mashed potato
#IrishShadesOfGrey | cmccrudden

Maureen couldnt get over how firm, well-formed and magenta it was. The aubergines were much better quality in Superquinn.
#IrishShadesOfGrey | mizz_adventure

'More, more!' she urged, as his sauce splashed on her steaming single! Pat really liked his new job at the chip shop
#IrishShadesOfGrey | Greadyfarmer

'My God, the length of it…' she purred. 'For certain,' sez he, 'twas a fine crop of carrots this year and no mistake'
#IrishShadesOfGrey | BerginPaul

'Open your eyes,' he whispered, 'time to show you my new crop.' Spuds. A whole acre. Biddy always loved a tillage farmer
#IrishShadesOfGrey | florNEWS

'Pull harder, Bridie!' he said, as her hands began to cramp … Jimmy hated when the carrots put up a fight
#IrishShadesOfGrey | Niallon

Irish Shades of Grey

Ripe, juicy plums were in her hand. He didn't
flinch when Mary said 'That one's very hard,' &
shrugged. 'Greengrocers eh?'
#IrishShadesOfGrey | Kitsgirl1

She began to gag on the meat feast that filled her
mouth. The jumbo breakfast roll was too much.
#IrishShadesOfGrey | jojogallagher1

She closed her lips around it, holding the base
firmly. Sucking and licking with delight. Nowt
like a Calippo for a hangover
#IrishShadesOfGrey | ashneary

She curled, twisted, to the touch of him. Oozing,
she was ready. 'Have ye any brown sauce for this
bacon sanwich, Mary?'
#IrishShadesOfGrey | TellyDubby

She felt guilty, but still decided to go ahead and
finger herself. 'It was me,' she told her family, 'I
took the last Rolo'
#IrishShadesOfGrey | SCRUNCH1E

She fumbled excitedly, her fingers quivering as
she hovered over the shiny packet of Tayto
#IrishShadesOfGrey | niamhhassell

She gazed down its long, sleek shaft. Her lips
parted with anticipation. Superquinn sausages
couldn't be bate.
#IrishShadesOfGrey | Carrier11

She gazed with a look of intent, then she opened
up … the car boot to reveal a box full of
sandwiches
#IrishShadesOfGrey | RyanCullen90

She groaned in pleasure, rolling her tongue
around the hot nuts. He got up to refill the
empty container at the bar.
#IrishShadesOfGrey | Sinead_McE

She hefted the warm, pale length of meat in her
hands. 'Ah, Clonakilty white pudding,' she
sighed. 'No finer mouthful.'
#IrishShadesOfGrey | PlashingVole

She knew he was a class act! He had a family
crest: two potatoes either side of an empty
Guinness bottle!
#IrishShadesOfGrey | haughtonk9

She looked longingly along the shaft. She longed
for the salty taste. Licking her lips, she asked for
vinegar too
#IrishShadesOfGrey | DiCCollins

Irish Shades of Grey

She loved licking the creamy white yummy drips from around the rim of his firm, hard cone. 'Get your own Teddy's,' he said
#IrishShadesOfGrey | Paulhughesgee

She made such a sharp face, and said 'It's too salty, I can't swallow it!' I said 'Oysters aren't cheap, woman!'
#IrishShadesOfGrey | d_boylan_charm

She pulled and pulled and, as the white cream shot out, she asked 'would you like a flake and syrup on that?'
#IrishShadesOfGrey | altoir

She pulled back the skin, slid the tip into her mouth and thought 'I love bananas!' as she bit into it.
#IrishShadesOfGrey | ThatJoeyFella

She put it in her mouth, licked and slobbered it until it erupted & dribbled down her chin. Ciara loved a good Choc Ice
#IrishShadesOfGrey | peterfbrennan

She ran her finger along its considerable length, and postioned her body for entry. Bridie loved a meaty footlong from Subway
#IrishShadesOfGrey | luvs2spooge84

She ran her hands up & down to warm it and get
it up, dying to put it in her mouth and have a
suck … of that Calippo
#IrishShadesOfGrey | Claireklly

She ran her tongue around the sticky opening,
savouring the sweetness. Jaysus, I love a
Cadbury's Creme Egg, she thought.
#IrishShadesOfGrey | Sinead_McE

She ripped them open & slid her hand in. As she
grabbed hold, she thought 'Jayz, there's feck all
Tayto in a bag nowadays'
#IrishShadesOfGrey | Piquero82

He shoved the whole thing into her mouth & felt
the gooey white cream explode. Cadbury Creme
Eggs, how do you eat yours?
#IrishShadesOfGrey | derekf03

She sucked it, rolled it around her tongue … The
climax was near; then exploded into ecstasy. She
loved an Emerald Choc Lime
#IrishShadesOfGrey | 7worldscollide

She sucked on it hard, she needed that creamy
goo in her throat. Natalie always bit the bottom
of her '99 ice-cream cone.
#IrishShadesOfGrey | finchcaddy

Irish Shades of Grey

She tasted a vague saltiness, a subtle hint of spices from far-off lands. These new Curried Chip Taytos were a winner.
#IrishShadesOfGrey | alanbourke

She teasingly sucked along the edges, then probed her tongue tentatively along the ridge of the purple ... Snack
#IrishShadesOfGrey | kezzamcfezza

She took it in her hand, firmly, not too tight, & gently pulled the skin back, excited to taste it! Mary loved a baked POTATO
#IrishShadesOfGrey | Adrianne24

She took two balls in her mouth and moaned in pleasure. This Chinese would ruin her weightwatchers.
#IrishShadesOfGrey | LyndaInNYC

She wanted it for so long. She stared at it. Anticipated its size, heat, taste... She bit, gagged. Ah, Spiceburger.
#IrishShadesOfGrey | TellyDubby

She wanted to suck it ... She was hot ... But Brid just couldn't get her mouth around those jumbo Mr Freeze's
#IrishShadesOfGrey | fionamb83

She was sizzling. And as he watched her, his arousal grew and couldn't be contained, as he hadn't had a decent fry for days.
#IrishShadesOfGrey | ronnyzoo

'She's loving this,' he thought to himself as Mary swallowed all of the white sticky goo that oozed out of his Creme Egg
#IrishShadesOfGrey | rochelle_07

'Spread it gently,' she said, as she passed him Dairygold from the fridge.
#IrishShadesOfGrey | Chloe_OD

'Swallow it all!' Don't get up from the table til you finish every last bit!'
#IrishShadesOfGrey | BuachaillDana2

'Take that, and that, and that. You love it don't you?' yelled Mick. 'I do,' said Teresa, placing each potato in her bag
#IrishShadesOfGrey | Damn_Street

The 12-inch length felt warm and soft in her hands. Nothing better than a large breakfast roll
#IrishShadesOfGrey | ronandusty

The cleft was dewed with moisture, plump and pink … he plunged the lemon inside the chicken
#IrishShadesOfGrey | abbygreen3

Irish Shades of Grey

The butcher gave Mrs O'Reilly some tongue as she leant over the counter. She grabbed his packet and bid him good day
#IrishShadesOfGrey | DameCrusty

The drops hit heat forming a mist of rising steam. She laughed, and her head spun as she shook the vinegar on her chips.
#IrishShadesOfGrey | crmagahy

The feisty Italian was clearly in charge. 'Tell me what you want,' she said with venom. 'Battered sausage,' Seamus replied.
#IrishShadesOfGrey | eoghanmchugh

The restraints hurt her wrists. She struggled, spat, howled, pleaded: 'I only trew a feckin' kebab in yer one's face, Guard'
#IrishShadesOfGrey | TellyDubby

The sour taste remained in Breda's mouth long after Frank had left. Never again would she suck his Tangfastics.
#IrishShadesOfGrey | SCRUNCH1E

The thick substance slithered down the front of her blouse. 'OMG,' she gasped. 'Go aisy pouring the mayo for feck's sake!'
#IrishShadesOfGrey | AnFearRuaGAA

Tom began to shake in orgasmic anticipation as a panting, red-faced Mary eased her grip. The spuds were finally mashed.
#IrishShadesOfGrey | Castleislander

Tom found Mary struggling with a tin of Heinz... 'You DID say you wanted to watch me flick a bean?!' she explained.
#IrishShadesOfGrey | LucyFur_70

'Twas white, bulging, barley held within its skin, ready for the taking. Jaysus she loved Clonakilty White Pudding
#IrishShadesOfGrey | TellyDubby

With two juicy breasts in his hands, he cheekily smiled at her and said, 'They gave me an extra breast in a bun, love'
#IrishShadesOfGrey | auzzie2me

With superb wrist action he beat it until whipped into a frenzy. Almost breathless, he said that the Angel Delight was ready
#IrishShadesOfGrey | hmageejnr

'You'd better go back in quickly while you still can,' said Mary. Tesco was only open for another ten minutes
#IrishShadesOfGrey | sherlockodile

Irish Shades of Grey

All those models showing off their talent in the mud have the watching men really excited. Hard to beat the ploughing!
#IrishShadesOfGrey | kencurtin

He looked at her with a wanting desire barely able to keep it together. Freshly sheared sheep never looked so hot
#IrishShadesOfGrey | burke_cb

Mary had never felt anything like this in her life … Pat must have set the electric fence on high this time
#IrishShadesOfGrey | AMacDulake

She began to breathe heavily … Thowing bales into the barn was heavy work.
#IrishShadesOfGrey | MorganFinucane

She jumped on top nervously. Then firm in a straddling position she thought 'it's been a while since I've hopped a gate'
#IrishShadesOfGrey | finnegan339

She pulled it faster & faster, harder & harder. Finally, the white stuff came pouring out. I did it, I milked my first cow!
#IrishShadesOfGrey | onyerbike69

She took a deep breath, and ordered him to 'get it in there nice and tight.' 'Sure how else do ye roll hay bales?' he replied.
#IrishShadesOfGrey | stickytoffeepup

When she saw the size of it, she moaned with anticipation and she wanted him to give it to her … His milk quota.
#IrishShadesOfGrey | rugbylane

All she could feel was the throbbing beneath her. She moved quickly to adjust her position … then reversed the tractor
#IrishShadesOfGrey | JeffHar73

As her legs were spread and the juices poured out, he could see it in her eyes … she was ready to calf
#IrishShadesOfGrey | gerluby

As the vibrations between her legs grew, she took a commanding grasp of the shaft and put the Massey Ferguson into gear.
#IrishShadesOfGrey | stephenfinn3

Don't be afraid to use your fingers! Get stuck in: rich, moist, best in the world. That Diarmuid Gavin knows his soil.
#IrishShadesOfGrey | TellyDubby

Irish Shades of Grey

Every chance, Tom would have his cock out!!!!
'Biggest cock in Ireland,' he boasted, as he put it
back in with the hens
#IrishShadesOfGrey | fergalcantwell

Frustration mounted with every stroke. Tug after
tug without response. Panic set in. 'I'll never get
the grass cut,' she sighed
#IrishShadesOfGrey | joeykell

Half asleep, he fumbled with the nipples as he
knew she was watching him. He caressed her tits,
beginning the milking
#IrishShadesOfGrey | LiamMcSOS

He spread Daisy just the way she liked … Any
minute now … A newborn calf
#IrishShadesOfGrey | ConorSwe

He had settled into a rhythm, he ploughed fast &
hard … nothing less would be accepted to win
the ploughing contest
#IrishShadesOfGrey | kylem17

He looked up, she was bent over in front of him,
sweating. He loved footing turf with Bridget
#IrishShadesOfGrey | BuachaillDana2

Paul Duggan

He slowly penetrated as she screamed, going deep inside. In an hour it was over, the calf was born to a healthy heiffer
#IrishShadesOfGrey |Ciara_BK

He spanked her gently with the rod in his hand. It was the only way to get that bastard cow into the shed.
#IrishShadesOfGrey | Patrick_Thorn

He took his shirt from the ground and wiped the sweat from his chest. 'Right, get me a bag, we'll start packing the turf'
#IrishShadesOfGrey | KevinIsCoolOK

He wrapped her up in the black, shiny material. It clinged in all the right places. 'Twas a fine day for baling hay
#IrishShadesOfGrey | Ankhyu

Her moans grew in intensity as he worked frantically behind her … Finally number 54 delivered a fine little bull calf
#IrishShadesOfGrey | Hellers76

It had been a while since she saw the lad! His head popped out. She enjoyed a bit of aul' haystack hide and seek.
#IrishShadesOfGrey | RavishinRick

Irish Shades of Grey

It was starting to hurt now, muscles burning,
pleading for him to stop. But feck it, he had to
get this tractor to start!
#IrishShadesOfGrey | pdhannan

'It's so BIG and so red and shiny,' Mary purred,
impressed. Yes, Padraig was shocking proud of his
new Massey Ferguson
#IrishShadesOfGrey | susankilkenny

Johnny cupped her backside gently as she bucked
and groaned – then helped guide the new baby
calf out.
#IrishShadesOfGrey | Shannairl

On her haunches, she blushed with inexperience
as his seed spilled through her fingers – these
spuds will never get planted
#IrishShadesOfGrey | Kitchen72

'Ouch,' she moaned. 'I won't be able to walk after
this!' Mary was exhausted, but glad to be nearly
finished with the bog
#IrishShadesOfGrey | ManusCoyle

Reaching between her legs, he found the swollen
heat. Her cream dripped from his fingers. Nuala,
the best cow of the herd
#IrishShadesOfGrey | dp_polo

She admired his strong, powerful legs, gasping as he effortlessly strode the floor. 'Tis a fine bullock,' she exclaimed
#IrishShadesOfGrey | leedalyire

She grabbed it and pulled gently, but still the white juice wouldn't come … milking a cow wasn't as easy as she thought….
#IrishShadesOfGrey | LucyFur_70

She rolled around the field, her leather coat resplendent. Her tongue went on forever. That cow really loved a good salt lick
#IrishShadesOfGrey | buzzoneill

She trembled as his hands ran down her parted legs, and she tensed at the vibrations. She hated being sheared
#IrishShadesOfGrey | Richy1137

'Suck it, suck it … G'wan … Almost … Now we're suckin Diesel!' said Cathal, as the tractor started on a cold winter's day
#IrishShadesOfGrey | Raytional

'Thats a nice large piece of equipment in between your legs,' she said, as the farmer got off the quad.
#IrishShadesOfGrey | FGinnity

Irish Shades of Grey

They were in full flow at this stage, up and down, hard and fast. The tractor's suspension dealt with the road well.
#IrishShadesOfGrey | auzzie2me

This isn't the big dirty ride I had in mind, thought Sarah wistfully as the Massey Ferguson trundled into Gort
#IrishShadesOfGrey | FachtnaK

She opened her mouth, sighing as it hit her tongue. Holy Moses. They could do with paprika on these communion wafers.
#IrishShadesOfGrey | kiki3387

A shiver ran down her spine. Goosebumps rose on her pale white skin, her nipples taut, & then she knew the heating was broke.
#IrishShadesOfGrey | joeman42

Pat held his sack tight as Mary reached for his perfectly formed balls. She pulled them out. God how they loved Bingo.
#IrishShadesOfGrey | joeman42

'No higher,' panted Mary … as Patrick pressed her button, she convulsed in excitement … Oh what fun bidding on Ebay
#IrishShadesOfGrey | Glamourpussmamo

'Tell me,' he said, his voice low and husky over the phone, 'What are you wearing?' 'Eh? Me clothes, u feckin gobshite.'
#IrishShadesOfGrey | CowboyJunkie

"Enter me quickly please,' Mary pleaded – eventually Sean relented and posted off her three star winning streak ticket
#IrishShadesOfGrey | STIGUCD

Everyone in a circle, sweating, blowing, puffing and panting, the rhythm taking hold of their bodies. The *Fleadh* was ninety!
#IrishShadesOfGrey | teaassasin

Face to face they stared as beads of sweat trickled down his lip. The tension filled the room… Was it step 1.2.3. or spin ?
#IrishShadesOfGrey | LiamButler3

He asked her to lay back, he was slowly getting closer to her mouth … 'A lot of plaque buildup, Mary, are you brushing?'
#IrishShadesOfGrey | McDanmc

He beckoned her to touch his pounding member and whispered, 'I banged me finger putting that feckin Ikea flat pack together.'
#IrishShadesOfGrey | burke_cb

Irish Shades of Grey

He came on her ass. 'Did you enjoy the ride, Pakky?' she asked. 'Not bad, Biddy, but I prefer the horse.'
#IrishShadesOfGrey | OhGamu

He had her up against the wall, ready to mount her. Says Sheila, 'You're not sticking that Linda Martin calendar up there!!'
#IrishShadesOfGrey | seanleonardart

He loved that her toes curled during it … she wished he'd give her time to take off her tights.
#IrishShadesOfGrey | johnnyf67

He slowly pulled off her Aran jumper. She was cold. She hid under the duvet.
#IrishShadesOfGrey | jimbosmyname

Her breathing quickened, heart racing, it looked so big and heavy. And Ryanair only allows10kg…
#IrishShadesOfGrey | Pruemagoo

He trembled with anticipation. '69?' I mumbled. 'BINGO! he roared. 'BINGO!' And shure he hadn't a bingo at all, the caffling.
#IrishShadesOfGrey | samrboland

He turned off the tv and leaned over her. She trembled. He uttered the words, 'Which bin has to go out, the green or blue?'
#IrishShadesOfGrey | RTReade

Paul Duggan

Mary blowing, Sean fingering, and sweat flowing
off them. Winning the flute & accordion duet at
the *fleadh* was the promise....
#IrishShadesOfGrey | teaassasin

Mary led the TV licence man upstairs by the
hand – he told her it'd been a long time since he
saw a 32-inch Bush.
#IrishShadesOfGrey | cecilbdeholy

Nuala wanted him to ravish her out on the lawn.
She'd put the Infant of Prague out tonight to
make sure of the weather.
#IrishShadesOfGrey | EiTechGuy

She always liked it from behind and she told him
so. 'Sure we always give the tetanus injection this
way, Mrs Murphy.'
#IrishShadesOfGrey | burke_cb

She fell onto his lap, and he spread her apart
inhaling deeply. *Ireland's Own* was a highlight of
his week!!
#IrishShadesOfGrey | RachelWade

She knew she had control, and he'd have to do
what she desired. Mammy's son always behaved
when she had the wooden spoon.
#IrishShadesOfGrey | mynameisMrSnrub

Irish Shades of Grey

She lay on her back poised, the summer breeze
gently rustling the barley. 'Jesus that's a grand
drying day,' she thought.
#IrishShadesOfGrey | spadetownboy

She mounted him bareback, dripping, panting –
riding him until his knees gave out. Mary loved
jockyback races on the beach.
#IrishShadesOfGrey | LauraKealy1

She moved her legs together, adjusting her skirt.
Jayz these Dunnes Stores changing rooms are
very pokey.
#IrishShadesOfGrey | Pruemagoo

She sat up, and looked him deep in the eye,
loving how nice and hard he was. 'Get off me
feckin ribs, Mary!' he screamed.
#IrishShadesOfGrey | onyerbike69

She wanted to treat him to something amazing to
mark their anniversary, so she went to Centra for
an allowance day special.
#IrishShadesOfGrey | kencurtin

She was nervous at first … It was big and long …
She had to try it. She went up and down on it.
She loves escalators now.
#IrishShadesOfGrey | CrazyCol91

She was the wettest she had ever been. It was
tight. She repositioned herself so he could enter.
The 8 a.m. Dart was the worst.
#IrishShadesOfGrey | LauraKealy1

Sile thanked Mick for the crossbar home from
the dance. 'Twas only as he cycled away she
noticed it was a ladies racer.
#IrishShadesOfGrey | cecilbdeholy

Soaking wet, legs flailing, head going, and the
tongue hanging out. Spot never liked being
washed, but it had to be done.
#IrishShadesOfGrey | teaassasin

'Stop!' she cried, 'the pain is too much.' He
pushed harder, harder. 'Listen, Lady, you're the
one who said you were a size 5.'
#IrishShadesOfGrey | PhilDonohue1

'Tell me if it hurts too much and I'll take it out,'
said the dentist.
#IrishShadesOfGrey | Lauragorman77

The erection was not quite what she imagined ...
Poor auld Seany's headstone was finally in place.
#IrishShadesOfGrey | onyerbike69

She felt herself lifting, relaxing, oozing with joy.
'Weee' she cried, 'these swings are the best'!
#IrishShadesOfGrey | karltipping

Irish Shades of Grey

There was a faint whiff of BO from Sile's
unshaved armpit. It looked like she had Don
King in a headlock.
#IrishShadesOfGrey | cecilbdeholy

They climaxed simultaneously as they looked
into the warm glow of the fire … in July!!!
#IrishShadesOfGrey | debbieoc21

In the aftermath, gently panting, she turned to
him, and whispered… 'My cousin's from your
Parish!'
#IrishShadesOfGrey | claireok_2000

A guilty scream escaped her lips as she writhed in
her seat to Santa Ponsa. She'd just realised she left
the immersion on
#IrishShadesOfGrey | SheenaMadden

After a luxurious bath, he threw her onto the
bed, crawled on top of her and said … 'Did you
turn off the immersion?'
#IrishShadesOfGrey | Gfunkmooney

Ah Gwan Gwan Gwan Gwan Gwan Gwan
Gwan Gwan Gwan Gwan Gwan Gwan Gwan
Gwan Gwan Gwan Gwan Gwan Gwan – *TÁ
MÉ AG TEACHT!*
#IrishShadesOfGrey | FiftyShadesEire

All he had in his trousers he rammed into her tight, inviting crack until she was full. Paudi loved trocaire boxes.
#IrishShadesOfGrey | Daithi74

All she could see was a big dick filling her gaze. That 60" telly Jim had bought was great for watching *Diagnosis Murder*
#IrishShadesOfGrey | GeordieWalrus

Any second! Wait! Wait! Wait! Yes, now … yes … now! BONG. BONG. BONG. The Angelus was a highlight of the day.
#IrishShadesOfGrey | TellyDubby

Apron on, down on her knees … as she got nearer to the rim, she began to gag. Mary hated cleaning toilets
#IrishShadesOfGrey | Gigibongi

As beads of sweat began to drip from her, she shouted, 'who left the immersion on?'
#IrishShadesOfGrey | jojogallagher1

As he guided his massive tool into her mouth, she let out a moan. 'One more tooth and we're done, Mary,' said the dentist
#IrishShadesOfGrey | ConorDowler

Irish Shades of Grey

As our fingers touched, I felt an odd, exhilarating shiver run through me – this was the first time I'd met Brendan Grace.
#IrishShadesOfGrey | OliverClare

As Paudie gazed gently into her mouth, he thought to himself 'Jesus this Amazon is some river....'
#IrishShadesOfGrey | Derekfallon

As she got out of the Bridal car w/ soul full of hope, she remembered getting out of the bath w/ a hole full of soap.
#IrishShadesOfGrey | DAMOSPOSTS

As she watched, he went up & down, up & down … limbs flailing with joy… Yes, @DustinOfficial was doing flapflaps again!
#IrishShadesOfGrey | NiallOK

As soon as he was on top, she pulled frantically, forcing him down. It was all about power and control. She loved swingboats
#IrishShadesOfGrey | Red_Regi

Belatedly, he slipped his pump inside. Looking up, he groaned as he realised that the price of petrol had gone up again
#IrishShadesOfGrey | LiamMcSOS

Bent over his knee, Sean pulled back the underwear. 'Mary, the child's nappy needs changing,' he said
#IrishShadesOfGrey | OccupyIreland

Do you have protection?' she whispers … 'I've a baseball bat in the back, but those lads haven't been around here in a while'
#IrishShadesOfGrey | PaulDuggan_

Bernie screamed, clutching the pillows, 'YES!! YES!!' … She matched 2 numbers on the lotto and won 8 quid
#IrishShadesOfGrey | RianMac

Breda slowly put her hand between her legs. She was moist at the touch. Well feck it, she had wet the bed again
#IrishShadesOfGrey | SCRUNCH1E

'Come around the back,' she whispered. He gasped. She'd never invited him to a lock-in at her Da's pub before.
#IrishShadesOfGrey | TellyDubby

'Come on, get the glove. Smear it all over me. Everywhere!' she screamed. Seán hated applying Mary's St Tropez….
#IrishShadesOfGrey | philipnolan1

Irish Shades of Grey

Dermot smiled as it slowly got harder. Soon he'd take her to new heights … his precast concrete stairs had almost set.
#IrishShadesOfGrey | woollywhite

'Do you want it hard or soft?' Sean asked. Mary trembled. 'Hard please.' So he didn't email, but printed the document instead
#IrishShadesOfGrey | SEVEfan1

'Do you want your auld lobby washed down, sunshine?' she asked breathlessly
#IrishShadesOfGrey | redmum

He had a horn on him that would pull a bullock from a bog
#IrishShadesOfGrey | kierancuddihy

Down, down, deeper and down. She couldn't believe what was happening to her. Her body squirmed … The ISAC was crashing.
#IrishShadesOfGrey | TellyDubby

Drip drip drip. Her mother had warned her about getting turned on, but she couldn't resist the temptation. The immersion.
#IrishShadesOfGrey | irishkangaroo

He softly whispered to her, 'Your eyes light up the night like a pair of Zetor headlamps.'
#IrishShadesOfGrey | IanFlavin

'Every stitch I have is wringing,' she moaned. 'Please, please, please … Buy me a fecking tumble dryer, would ya?'
#IrishShadesOfGrey | SharonOwensAuth

'Feck off, I'm a lesbian,' sez yer wan to the lairy lad. His interest rose. 'Feckin brill … how are things in Beirut?'
#IrishShadesOfGrey | TellyDubby

'Give it to me now!' she roared urgently. 'I'm coming!' he said, as he stuck his hand around the door with the loo roll
#IrishShadesOfGrey | NursepollyRgn

'Harder, harder!' she screamed, as the sweat rolled down Billy's eyes as he hammered her … nails into a lovely shelf
#IrishShadesOfGrey | DaleHealy_

'Harder,' Seamus said to Bríd, down on her knees … 'Stains won't come out of a carpet without a bit of elbow grease'
#IrishShadesOfGrey | eciRhannaH

He almost choked as the priest forced it into his mouth, the taste more vulgar than he feared. 'Father, that wine is shite'
#IrishShadesOfGrey | Nialler67

Irish Shades of Grey

He came four times an hour between morning &
lunchtime … the egg man wasn't going to stop
calling until he got paid.
#IrishShadesOfGrey | iGarageIreland

He had what she wanted and made her beg for it.
She'd enjoy it, and she went wild when he gave it
to her. Westlife tickets
#IrishShadesOfGrey | martynrosney

He knocked firmly on the door and enticed her.
'Open wide, see what's on the other side.' … She
always loved Bosco
#IrishShadesOfGrey | stokesie84

He spent all his time deep in a box with a fist
inside him. Bosco was a legend.
#IrishShadesOfGrey | paulyc87

He sucked on his middle finger, stuck it up and
smiled in satisfaction as he shouted 'Up yours!' to
the riot police.
#IrishShadesOfGrey | JonMuzza1

He took deep breaths, prepared to slip inside.
'Sorry bud, ye're not comin in here wit dem
runners! said the bouncer.
#IrishShadesOfGrey | tom_cos

Paul Duggan

He took her hand and promised to be gentle.
The taste of latex in her mouth made her gag.
Bríd hated going to the dentist.
#IrishShadesOfGrey | ornatoolbox

He took out his glistening flute. She took it
gently, brought it to her mouth and blew.
'Gorgeous tone,' she said.
#IrishShadesOfGrey | sebaldfan

He was good at fingering. She was brilliant at
blowing to create a sweet melody. They were
both excellent flute players
#IrishShadesOfGrey | Eileen_Brennan

He was in front of her now: tanned, tight, ready
for action. 'Are you paying too much for your
broadband?' he asked.
#IrishShadesOfGrey | TellyDubby

He was rubbing furiously, his hand cramping as
she reached euphoria. Nothing bate watching
him clean the windows
#IrishShadesOfGrey | discosunbeams

He was sprawled on the couch. Down on her
knees, she lowered the zip. 'Feck it,' she moaned
'pass me the lighter'
#IrishShadesOfGrey | derryo

Heat enveloped her body & as a bead of sweat
ran down her back she knew doing a boils wash
in the kitchen was a bad idea!
#IrishShadesOfGrey | daithi_g

Her hand quivered as she reached for his
member... ship card. It was off to the cash and
carry with her.
#IrishShadesOfGrey | kenmooney

Her heart was pounding, bereft, what to do, wet
and sweaty. Up he flew after a text with a Tesco
points card
#IrishShadesOfGrey | Kitsgirl1

Her nickname was 'The Bowling Ball' because
she took 3 fingers and loved getting fucked down
an alleyway
#IrishShadesOfGrey | Sean_Corr

Her underwear was wet as he pulled the rope …
There's great drying outside today, she thought,
as the clothes line hoisted
#IrishShadesOfGrey | PaudieNewstalk

His eyes met hers. The burning in her loins
increased … she had to ask him … 'Is this cream
good for Cystitis?'
#IrishShadesOfGrey | Claredaisy

His skin was raw from the scratches of her nails, the harder it went the deeper she got. Chinese burns, bad idea
#IrishShadesOfGrey | noeleen81

I came out of it hot, sweaty, emotional and in bits. Oh Jaysus I was in bits – Michael on the Westlife gig.
#IrishShadesOfGrey | Shannon2Wel

'I like it nice n stiff,' says she. 'Stiff?' says I. 'Stiff!' says she. 'You'd be better off usin Mr Percil n starch,' says I.
#IrishShadesOfGrey | davebolger

'I want it hot and strong and dark,' she whimpered. 'No, Mrs Doyle. It's not #IrishShadesOfTay. It's #IrishShadesOfGrey you eejit.'
#IrishShadesOfGrey | PlashingVole

'I want you to tie me down for 18 months and treat me like dirt,' she said. The man from Vodafone got the contract out....
#IrishShadesOfGrey | philipnolan1

I was nervous as she slowly came toward me, breathing heavily. I rose quickly, and gave the auld one my seat on the bus
#IrishShadesOfGrey | gartarr

Irish Shades of Grey

I'm comin! I'm comin! Jesus, I'm only five minutes late, Boss!
#IrishShadesOfGrey | GerryOMahony

'I'm nearly in, nearly there, God it's tight,' as he eventually fished the car keys from the side of the seat....
#IrishShadesOfGrey | rjwin1

In and out and in and out but no joy for her … the junkie had already ruined all her veins!
#IrishShadesOfGrey | leduigs

In out, in out, in out, her body ached but she could not stop. She loved doing the hokey pokey
#IrishShadesOfGrey | NuggetDave

'Is that a mouse hole down there to be sure?' he asked. I replied 'Feck off! That's how the first 9 kids happened!'
#IrishShadesOfGrey | haughtonk9

It almost reached the ground, she wrapped her fingers around it and tugged. Oh, how she loved ringing the Angelus.
#IrishShadesOfGrey | richardadalton

It feels like I'm on my knees front of a different man every week, Mary thought to herself. Yet another new priest
IrishShadesOfGrey | GeordieWalrus

It gave her so much pleasure as he slid in and out
of the box vigorously … she loved watching
Bosco
#IrishShadesOfGrey | markjsobrien

It glided in, but there was a hitch. 'We need some
lubrication,' she said. 'Bloody Sliderobes, after all
we spent on them….'
#IrishShadesOfGrey | TellyDubby

'It reminds me of his,' said Bridie looking at the
carrot. 'What, the length or the width?' asked
Ruth. 'No, the fuckin dirt'
#IrishShadesOfGrey | IrelandUncut

It took her hours to come. There were some
leaves on the tracks
#IrishShadesOfGrey | OlafTyaransen

It was long, hard and too much for her to take in
at once. Maths paper one was particularly
difficult this year.
#IrishShadesOfGrey | Sean_is_Deadly

'It's agony,' she moaned, 'take it out, please, I
can't stand it.' 'Ok, open wide, let's take a look,'
said the dentist
#IrishShadesOfGrey | Lauragorman77

Irish Shades of Grey

'It's my new toy Buzz. I leave him beside my bed,
along with my old toy I used to play with
Woody,' the *Toy Story* fan said
#IrishShadesOfGrey | kbkevinbyrne

'It's really hotting up now,' she thought, right
before she realised she'd left the immersion on.
#IrishShadesOfGrey | HearneAoife

'Let's film our lovemaking,' Sean said. 'We could
call it *Porn On The Fourth Of July*.'
#IrishShadesOfGrey | pjmccluskey

Mary always felt giddy this time of the month.
Even Tom's smelly feet didn't put her off. Bless
Children's Allowance Day
#IrishShadesOfGrey | MiriamDonohoe

Mary and Pat moved as one, sweat glistening off
their bodies. Mary screams in ecstasy, 'Best Saw
Doctors gig ever, Pat!'
#IrishShadesOfGrey | padraigco

Mary gripped the balls tighter – so round and
hard, even after five decades. She loved saying
the Rosary.
#IrishShadesOfGrey | Gough_Cat

Paul Duggan

Mary gripped the long, thick, hard wood with both hands … 'Hup ya boy ya!' she cried, as she slid down the banister
#IrishShadesOfGrey | sharkcub

Mary held her breath as he slowly inched in her back door … Father Molloy wasn't the same since his hip replacement
#IrishShadesOfGrey | chiminaaaaa

Mary purposefully took possession of the hardness between his thighs. Not a chance she was missing *Fair City* again tonight
#IrishShadesOfGrey | SheenaMadden

Mary sucked on a big one. The spider was no match for her and her hoover.
#IrishShadesOfGrey | jojogallagher1

Mary tugged, twisting her fingers, wringing, pulling, until the liquid rushed out. She then hung it on the clothes-line.
#IrishShadesOfGrey | jackyoulate

Mary was ecstatic as Mike hammered his wood into her lush meadow. She had been waiting for new fencing poles
#IrishShadesOfGrey | ShaneFitz1991

Irish Shades of Grey

Mick and Mary turned him on in their bed every Friday night: Gay Byrne.
#IrishShadesOfGrey | DanielCollins85

Mildred giggled coquettishly. Pushing Sean's hands away, she leaped out of bed to turn John Paul II's face to the wall.
#IrishShadesOfGrey | IAreLizz

'Mossy, could we just be platonic?' 'If that involves riding I'm up for it.'
#IrishShadesOfGrey | DAMOSPOSTS

'My God you are so hard and thick...' said Mary, trembling in the arms of Mike Tyson...
#IrishShadesOfGrey | Derekfallon

Next month's specials for Children's Allowance Day are handcuffs, whips, chains and 3 for 2 on assorted bondage gear!
#IrishShadesOfGrey | PhilDonohue1

'Nice perfume,' says Tom to Tess, 'what's it called?' '*Komm zu Mir* [come to me]' says Tess. 'Doesn't smell like come to me,' says Tom
#IrishShadesOfGrey | DAMOSPOSTS

Night fell, once again she could indulge her need for rubber & velcro. Between the sheets the hot-water bottle felt so good.
#IrishShadesOfGrey | famron

'No, Pat,' she said, 'the lads were only having you on. You won't need the flashlight to find me G spot'
#IrishShadesOfGrey | DavidOShelton

'No,' she gasped as he moved hungrily towards her, 'not tonight. It's Saturday. I've had me bath & changed the sheets, pet.
#IrishShadesOfGrey | JenStevensDub

Nuala stuck her finger in the hole & blew hard, wiping it on her blouse after. She stuck it in. The CD didn't skip again
#IrishShadesOfGrey | stemannion

Nuala thrashed, and thrashed and thrashed. This hall rug wouldn't clean itself
#IrishShadesOfGrey | cmccrudden

'Oh for the love of god they've been at it all night!' screamed the nun in excitement, as she checked her twitter timeline
#IrishShadesOfGrey | Glamourpussmamo

'Oh please,' she begged, desperate for relief. He stared down at her dispassionately. 'Sorry luv, jax's out of order.'
#IrishShadesOfGrey | catspjs13

Irish Shades of Grey

'OMG its so focking long and hard, Seán!' Bríd
screamed. 'Yes indeed, but nobody said Honours
Maths was supposed to be easy'
#IrishShadesOfGrey | KevinDenny

On her knees and obedient once more, she
suppressed a submissive thrill. He should never
know how much she loved Mass.
#IrishShadesOfGrey | PlashingVole

On her knees, excitement filled her. She opened
her mouth with anticipation, chanting 'Hail
Mary' along with the priest.
#IrishShadesOfGrey | Keyrahhx

On her knees, he whispered instructions into her
box. She was a bad girl and hadn't been to
confession since Christmas
#IrishShadesOfGrey | Red_Regi

'Open Wide,' he whispered, in halitosis laden
breath. She mumbled 'No.' Christ, she thought,
 I need a new dentist
#IrishShadesOfGrey | DiamondsIRL

Paddy came up from under the duvet and said
'Brenda, I think you should diet.' 'Why, what
colour is it now?' replied Brenda
#IrishShadesOfGrey | GrahamAByrne

Paddy's raised hand silenced Mary. Her body trembled with anticipation. 'Hush,' he said, '*The Sunday Game* is starting.'
#IrishShadesOfGrey | JoMcArdle

Pat realised Peggy was a large lady as she took off her G rope
#IrishShadesOfGrey | GrahamAByrne

'Please, give it to me, give it to me,' she urged him desperately. Twas always hard getting the Bus Éireann child ticket
#IrishShadesOfGrey | Shannon2Wel

She bent over one more time, yearning to feel the heat and warmth it warmth it would give … She reached down, and cut the turf
#IrishShadesOfGrey | chrisplee

She checked out his package, it was huge & she was getting it, then some dope skipped the queue. Bad day workin 4 AnPost!
#IrishShadesOfGrey | rizzoboogiestar

She closed her lips and blew softly. Her fingerwork was incredible. Mountains of Pomeroy sounded beautiful on tin whistle.
#IrishShadesOfGrey | seanboneill

Irish Shades of Grey

She collapsed, exhausted, exhilarated, for the
third time, as he started again. Mary pleaded
'Not another siege of Ennis!'
#IrishShadesOfGrey | KieranSexton82

She demanded it time and time again, so he took
her up the aisle.
#IrishShadesOfGrey | MoynihanBrendan

She eyed its length, her eyes filled with want
and desire. Her lips parted. 'How much for
the shillelagh?'
#IrishShadesOfGrey | queenofpots

She licked her finger and deftly flicked to
Wednesday's TV listing in the RTÉ Guide.
#IrishShadesOfGrey | 86thLeinster

She gasped at the speed of the rhythmic thrusting
of his hand, the sound of his uilleann pipes
moves her still
#IrishShadesOfGrey | Richy1137

She got on her knees, opened wide and put out
her tongue. It made her feel heavenly. It was the
best communion she ever had!
#IrishShadesOfGrey | jimbosmyname

She made a mint out of her lady garden
#IrishShadesOfGrey | DAMOSPOSTS

She grabbed d knob, pulled as hard as she cud, heart jumping wit excitement. Never tawt she'd spin d wheel on *Winning Streak*
#IrishShadesOfGrey | MikOmani

She held her breath. The sense of danger was too much to take. Will they notice that she has 11 items in her basket....
#IrishShadesOfGrey | PhilDonohue1

She held his gaze and chewed her lip. He parted his lips to speak: 'Jaysus, Dymphna, is that cold sore back again?'
#IrishShadesOfGrey | JuniperJools

She held it tight and pushed it back and forth, the pressure always on constantly, sucking it all up. She loved her new Hoover
#IrishShadesOfGrey | Cazza27

She kept pulling it hard, jerking at it again and again as it remained stiff. Eventually the window blinds came loose.
#IrishShadesOfGrey | 1BrianDoherty

She lay down on the silk sheets and shivered as he leaned over her. 'I think it's time for the electric blanket again.'
#IrishShadesOfGrey | RosemaryMacCabe

Irish Shades of Grey

She lay in her lingerie on the bed & begged 'ANAL!!! Why are you so bleedin' ANAL?' as he ironed the pillowcase.
#IrishShadesOfGrey | KarlsTRIPattoni

She licked her lips in anticipation. He slipped off his jacket and she thought; 'One down, thirty-nine to go!'
#IrishShadesOfGrey | RuDoran

She longed for him to dominate her but, with all the feckin' cutbacks, he was only moderately controlling.
#IrishShadesOfGrey | SeanX3

She longed to reveal her innermost desires to him, but she hesitated. Sensing her fear, he spoke. 'Talk to Joe,' he said.
#IrishShadesOfGrey | tcomerford

She looked with apprehension at the small metal object. 'Come on,' says he, 'I'll show you how to bleed a radiator'
#IrishShadesOfGrey | _Marie45

She marvelled at the purple, veiny, throbbing head and wondered if the bishop's mitre wasn't a tad tight for him.
#IrishShadesOfGrey | kavatarz

She moaned as he ran his fingernails down her back. That's the last time I buy washing powder from Aldi, she thought.
#IrishShadesOfGrey | sharonjwalsh

She moaned constantly, even started to drool randomly during it. I should have never let her agree to that frontal lobotomy
#IrishShadesOfGrey | kbkevinbyrne

She moved towards him slowly, gently kneeled down and opened her mouth. The priest gave her communion and blessed her.
#IrishShadesOfGrey | ChristianHughes

She opened her mouth and got ready to take it … The communion wafer at mass this week was tense
#IrishShadesOfGrey | KayDeeStafford

She opened her mouth, wide as she could. He inserted, sure to give it a filling. She shrieked. Mary hated the dentist.
#IrishShadesOfGrey | Irish_Biddy

She opened wide to receive it and he placed it slowly on her tongue. It had a familiar texture. 'Body of Christ,' he said.
#IrishShadesOfGrey | TommyyCampbell

Irish Shades of Grey

She panted, sweat trickling down her body, and
he slowly removed her from the harness. It was
hard tonight ... her 1st TRX class
#IrishShadesOfGrey | Jewlieann

She played, fondled & pressed it with her hands,
tighter and tighter ... bang! The explosion. She
smiled. Mary loved bubblewrap.
#IrishShadesOfGrey | kbkevinbyrne

She quivered as I stroked her thighs. 'Take me in
the shower, Sean.' I whispered to her, 'Wait till I
heat up the immersion....'
#IrishShadesOfGrey | PaudieNewstalk

She quivered with anticipation. 119 seconds
seemed like an eternity. She grabbed it in her
hand and brought it closer
#IrishShadesOfGrey | Hoppalicious

She rubbed it hard and long. She wouldn't stop
until she finished it off. Finally Ma got the mud
off me school trousers.
#IrishShadesOfGrey | Mark2bin

She saw him across the dance floor! He was
stood where all the other blokes were! She with
the girls!
#IrishShadesOfGrey | haughtonk9

She slipped it between her legs, feeling the
warmth on her thighs. She loves a good hot-
water bottle
#IrishShadesOfGrey | CKeegan24

She slowly took the cigarette from his lips and
whispered, 'Can I nip this for later?'
#IrishShadesOfGrey | rodge73

She stared him in the eye as he pounded hard.
Faster & deeper. Relentless. She loved watching
him put those fence posts in
#IrishShadesOfGrey | mikebromham

She started panting heavily & more frequently as
she rubbed her fingers vigorously through her
wet … cups in the sink :O
#IrishShadesOfGrey | DarrenBullman

She turned around slowly, looked deep into
his eyes and gripped him firmly … 'Peace be
with you.'
#IrishShadesOfGrey | rachelmrgn

She waited & waited – it was the waiting drove
her to frenzy, not yet, not yet … And then:
'Welcome to the *Late Late Show*'
#IrishShadesOfGrey | SeanMcP

Irish Shades of Grey

She waited silently, he moved closer and forced it upon her. She hated it when the priest put the communion in her mouth
#IrishShadesOfGrey | CaptainSteveFTW

She was kneeling, head bowed, the atmosphere was tense & boy was it hard. It had been a while since her last confession
#IrishShadesOfGrey | Jewlieann

She was looking her best and out for one thing only! Best in show at the local vintage rally!
#IrishShadesOfGrey | smceneaneyirl

She was on her knees in front of him. Looking up, she slowly lowered the zip and pulled them out. 'Hail Mary....'
#IrishShadesOfGrey | davebolger

She was soaking wet and excited. He was pitching a tent, just looking at her. It was the start of yet another Oxegen.
#IrishShadesOfGrey | Sean_is_Deadly

She wasn't sure she could take it a third time, but might it be even better? Could Jedward finally win the Eurovision?
#IrishShadesOfGrey | EiTechGuy

'Spread it all over my face.' She lay back, ready and willing, exhilarated by the free make-up samples in Brown Thomas.
#IrishShadesOfGrey | eleanor_rosney

'Spread them,' he ordered, roughly. Nervously, she spread them wide … there was no doubt her full house beat his pair of kings.
#IrishShadesOfGrey | maryroche

Sweat beaded on his brow as he thrust it in … there was a metallic clang as his shovel hit rock.
#IrishShadesOfGrey | CainUnabel

Sweat dripped from their writhing bodies until they finished, breathless and spent. The Riverdance hornpipes are a killer.
#IrishShadesOfGrey | ederoiste

Sweat trickled from his brow. He continued with force, in and out, his body aching. 'Aha! Try flushing her now,' he said.
#IrishShadesOfGrey | Irish_Biddy

'Take me now!' she urged, the desire evident in her deep blue eyes. 'I'll take you to Dunnes after the football,' he replied.
#IrishShadesOfGrey | davewall01

'Take me, take me now!' demanded Derbhla, 'or we'll miss 12 mass.'
#IrishShadesOfGrey | coriordan

'That was the best ride I've ever had…' said Mary, gasping for breath. 'Tis a pity Funderland only comes once a year.'
#IrishShadesOfGrey | sherlockodile

The black one was so big, and looked ready to spill its load. Fionnuala must put the wheelie bin out in the morning.
#IrishShadesOfGrey | LyndaInNYC

The fear. Oh my god. What was in store? She trembled, a virgin, couldn't find the words. Summer camp *as Gaeilge* awaited….
#IrishShadesOfGrey | TellyDubby

There was only one thing on her mind. Would he think her less of a woman for asking 'Who's taking the horse to France?'
#IrishShadesOfGrey | deedles2010

The sound of ripping material pierced the silence. 'That's the last feckin top I buy in Penneys!' screamed Áine.
#IrishShadesOfGrey | SpacemanPat

The touch from the ribbed rubber sent her temperature soaring. damn hot-water bottle had fallen out of its towel again.
#IrishShadesOfGrey | mynewhero

'Tits like melons,' he said. 'And nuts and seeds an all,' she replied.
#IrishShadesOfGrey | Korhomme

Tommy poured his load all over Bridey's buns. That's the last time he will bring a cement mixer into the kitchen.
#IrishShadesOfGrey | paulgaillimh

Tugging at the dog collar, she demanded swift punishment. 'OK,' he sighed, 'I'll hear your Confession.'
#IrishShadesOfGrey | PlashingVole

'Who knew 3.5 inches could bring so much joy?' she joked with her friends as she handed over her credit card in BTs.
#IrishShadesOfGrey | Gigibongi

'Who needs whips & handcuffs when you have a 3-foot length of wavin pipe and some bailing twine?' PJ asked.
#IrishShadesOfGrey | seanaoleary

Irish Shades of Grey

With every deeper lunge her moans increased to a scream. 'I really must replace that broken bed-spring' he thought….
#IrishShadesOfGrey | cliffsull

Would ye like some lube with that now? Are ye sure? Ah go on ya will. Ah go on. Ah you will, gowon.
#IrishShadesOfGrey | KatiCut

'YES! YES! YES!' she screamed, as she revealed 3 stars on a Winning Streak scratchcard
#IrishShadesOfGrey | RaraRortune

He couldn't stop thinking about muff … he enjoyed his time in Donegal
#IrishShadesOfGrey | DaithiMeath

He rubbed her beads between his fingers and she felt transformed. Rosary beads blessed, Mary knew this Lourdes trip was worth it.
#IrishShadesOfGrey | RachelWade

She put her hand around it and pulled excitedly. She was a mad one for the slots in Bundoran
#IrishShadesOfGrey | seanboneill

She longed for it so much it consumed her dreams, it was sooo tempting, but there is only a week left of lent till KitKat.
#IrishShadesOfGrey | RachelWade

At full speed he thrust forward, unsure it would even fit in this narrow passage. Roads in Louth were getting ridiculous.
#IrishShadesOfGrey | paulsmaroon924

'Get the handcuffs,' he said. 'Oh, big man in your uniform,' she cried. I hate working nights in Temple Bar, he thought.
#IrishShadesOfGrey | Liam_Geraghty

He had screwed thirty girls in one night. He really shouldn't have rigged the Rose of Tralee results.
#IrishShadesOfGrey | seanboneill

He slathered her in his thick, white paste. They were going to need factor 50 now that the sun was out in Courtown
#IrishShadesOfGrey | rochfora

He wasn't fooling me with that rubbish about his cock being the real Blarney Stone! And as for kissing it!
#IrishShadesOfGrey | haughtonk9

'I am so wet, I have never been so wet before.' 'Well you shouldn't have come to Donegal on holidays,' he replied.
#IrishShadesOfGrey | cathalmac

Irish Shades of Grey

'I wake up to your dong every morning, over and
over,' she purred, watching the Shandon Bells
#RebelShadesOfGrey
#IrishShadesOfGrey | TomMcCarthyCork

It was like nothing she had done before. Bending
over backwards and going down to kiss the
Blarney Stone
#IrishShadesOfGrey | SophieWalsh5

It went deeper than she ever imagined, and when
she closed her eyes she felt dizzy with excitement.
Ailwee Cave was class.
#IrishShadesOfGrey | Red_Regi

Martin's body tensed, his heart raced, his eyes
widened; it was the first time he had been taken
up the Giant's Causeway.
#IrishShadesOfGrey | Fullthrostle

Mary couldn't resist it. 'Jesus!' she cried, 'it's just
so big and dark!' It was her first time entering the
Port Tunnel.
#IrishShadesOfGrey | doctorjr

She hitched her skirt, he twanged her strings,
their voices began to rise together. Bunratty night
was always a hit.
#IrishShadesOfGrey | TellyDubby

She was tired and dripping but couldn't turn back. To do it so quickly with so many was a pleasant pain. Croagh Patrick
#IrishShadesOfGrey | Red_Regi

Tears streaming down her face, she had never been so wet in her life ... perhaps it was time for flood prevention in Douglas.
#IrishShadesOfGrey | ssfermoy

They really liked it hot and sticky. You can't beat crème brûlée after the roast beef in Barry's hotel before Croker.
#IrishShadesOfGrey | clarevirtually

They rolled, they swung, they rocked. A flurry of noise and grinding. This Cork-Dublin train is shite, thought PJ.
#IrishShadesOfGrey | colm_ryan

They were both sweaty and hot. They panted until, finally together, they made it to the summit.. Of Croagh Patrick
#IrishShadesOfGrey | Susie_2Z

Trembling with a burning desire, she leaned backwards, grabbed the railing with both hands, and kissed the Blarney Stone....
#IrishShadesOfGrey | onlyalexhayden

Irish Shades of Grey

Twas the most romantic of first dates. 15 pints, followed by a fumble in the corner of Coppers and a Rick's burger. Heaven.
#IrishShadesOfGrey | yvonneredmond

'You're so tight,' he said. 'I'm from Cavan,' she replied.
#IrishShadesOfGrey | mickbagnall

'Lob it into me, boss! screamed Bridy. She was about to discover what a square ball was.
#IrishShadesOfGrey | wasteofgoodskin

He'd been suspicious for while, but seeing her blistered bum he let fly – 'That's the fucking bike-to-work scheme for you!'
#IrishShadesOfGrey | sylmeulmeester

'Faster! Faster, Johnny!' she screamed, as her horse closed up to the finish line.
#IrishShadesOfGrey | BatmanAkaRobyn

'Give it to me! Give it to me now!' … But no way would the corner forward pass the ball.
#IrishShadesOfGrey | aisfennin

He lay between her legs, she tensed up, there were vibrations and shaking, she screamed, he pushed, tobogganing was great!!!
#IrishShadesOfGrey | Adomackno1965

He put his hand gently up her skirt. 'Darling,'
she said, 'control yourself – this is poker we're
playing....'
#IrishShadesOfGrey | Derekfallon

He sat there, on edge, staring downwards,
watching, waiting as it bobbed up & down
rhythmically. Then, she bit! #fishing
#IrishShadesOfGrey | cairotango

He slowly circled his finger around, enticing,
teasing, then firmly pressed down … What a
rush. He loved Knick Knacks.
#IrishShadesOfGrey | EdelChanMurphy

He slowly got down on his hands and knees,
hoping it would be over soon … He hated doing
press-ups in training
#IrishShadesOfGrey | CrazyCol91

Her sweaty thighs tightened around his warm
body. She panted, screaming 'Faster, you bastard!'
Mary won the Donkey Derby
#IrishShadesOfGrey | VainMann

In a longing embrace, he realised this could be
the one … the one goal which could win them
the league cup!
#IrishShadesOfGrey | smceneaneyirl

Irish Shades of Grey

It felt smooth, firm and long in her hands. 'God,' said the Camogie girl, 'tis hard to bate a good hurley….'
#IrishShadesOfGrey | AnFearRuaGAA

Just put in, stick it in there, just breathe, take your time, I'm so close, she thought as she had van Persie as first scorer
#IrishShadesOfGrey | DecFM104

Knowing she had no time to come up for air, Mary resisted the urge to gag, and finished first in the bog snorkelling race
#IrishShadesOfGrey | Red_Regi

She grasped the stiff object and pulled on it. She squealed in pleasure. Mary had clinched the camogie championship!
#IrishShadesOfGrey | EamonnG19

She gripped it for the first time. With the balls in front of her face, she took one deep breath & skilfully potted the red
#IrishShadesOfGrey | seanleonardart

She knew length was important. It was all she could think about since taking golf lessons.
#IrishShadesOfGrey | Red_Regi

She took a hold of his shaft in her trembling hands. 'That's a lovely hurl, Seanie,' she sighed.
#IrishShadesOfGrey | TheHorse75

She was raw from it. Exhausted, wasted, she yearned for the end. The pain, the foul language, the excess camogie was hell.
#IrishShadesOfGrey | TellyDubby

Wow, nobody can stop this guy! How has he managed to stay up this long? she wondered. It's Ronaldo for f**k sake!
#IrishShadesOfGrey | DecFM104

Anne-Marie gasped in disbelief as the sticky white drops fell about her face and neck. 'Sure it's too cold to snow!'
#IrishShadesOfGrey | DampFox

'Give it to me! I'm so fucking wet, give it to me now!!' 'Fuck off, this is my umbrella!'
#IrishShadesOfGrey | Shagwaable

He gazed upon her, dripping wet, standing in front of him. 'Jesus, Mary, would ya come in outta the rain for god's sake?'
#IrishShadesOfGrey | Sean_Eastman

'It's so incredibly wet,' Francois muttered. 'Didn't I tell you it never stops raining here?' said Mary.
#IrishShadesOfGrey | mangofever

Irish Shades of Grey

He sank in another inch, rubber constricting against his skin. 'Bloody wellies, bloody mud, bloody Summer,' he thought.
#IrishShadesOfGrey | jodyronaldson

'I'm dripping wet,' she sighed. 'Bloody Irish summers....'
#IrishShadesOfGrey | kavatarz

'I'm so wet!' Biddy cried. 'Me too, absolutely drenched to the core,' responded Annie. 'That's an Irish summer for yez.'
#IrishShadesOfGrey | KatiCut

'I'm soooo wet,' she moaned. 'That's June in Ireland for ya.'
#IrishShadesOfGrey | clogheentipp

It has been recorded that june has been the wettest june since 1910, all because of a book.
#IrishShadesOfGrey | Lols19O9O8

'It's so wet, dewey and dark. I want you to come inside now!! ... You'll catch pneumonia in this weather!'
#IrishShadesOfGrey | Jandyman95

Mary sat carefully, her backside red and sensitive. She blushed, remembering: she had fallen asleep in the sun again.
#IrishShadesOfGrey | catspjs13

'Oh god, I need you right now, I'm soaking wet!'
she whispered, searching the wardrobe for the aul
wellies.
#IrishShadesOfGrey | Keyrahhx

'Oh you're so wet,' he moaned. 'Yes,' she said,
ruefully. 'I can't believe I left my umbrella at
home today…!'
#IrishShadesOfGrey | clicky_here

She deeply exhaled as he finished caressing her
soaking carpet. 'There's bad flood damage here,
Maeve. May ring the council.'
#IrishShadesOfGrey | imsodoherty

She was so wet, she blushed while smothering a
giggle. It was her fault for wearing summer
clothes in Ireland in July.
#IrishShadesOfGrey | bojitsu